THE LEHIGH
HAUNTING

DONNA PARISH-BISCHOFF

Editor: Christopher DiCesare

Front Cover Illustration: Doreen Skolnick

Book Consultant: Donna Davies

DEDICATION

I would like to thank and dedicate this book to so many wonderful family members.

To my husband John, thank you for all of your encouragement and love. Thanks to our fur-babies, and to friends both old and new.

Thanks to those who gave me the courage and regular support to write this book. I would like to add an important 'thank you' to my sister Doreen who also lived through these experiences and to my brother in law, Drew, for his devoted advice in the arts. To my parents and my brother, Larry, who are all up in Heaven: hopefully I'm making you proud! I miss you all - and our talks and sharing cups of coffee – so very much! To my sister-in law Gerry and my niece, Nicole, for whom I know the substance of the book is not their 'cup of tea', thank you for bearing with me as I convey this story.

For the longest time I never dared to dream that this project would grow feet and walk...I knew it had the spine, but the feet were a long time in coming.

Finally, I also dedicate this book to all those who have a story of a haunting that they feel they could never speak of. I hand you this torch and say: "Run with it!" my friend …

Don't feel that no one will believe you, or help you. If you are going through a haunting, create a journal and then do your research!

And to anyone who holds this labor of love and determination in their hands, feel free to send me an e-mail, drop me a note, or ask me a question. I would love to hear from you!

Vampirella67@yahoo.com

ACKNOWLEDGMENTS

I would like to take a minute to thank those who have helped me get to this point of this second edition of *The Lee Avenue Haunting*. As with everything have its bumps and bruises and ups and downs. But with the help of some "key" people this was a possibility to make this book an even better read.

Many of the readers and fans that read my first edition wrote me. Some sharing their experiences with the paranormal and some sharing their disappointment in what they thought my first book was. I listened to all of the reviews. The good, the bad as well as the ugly. In hopes to redeem myself to the readers the and see if they are forgiving, I sought after a new editor.

I would like to give a big hand and thank you to Christopher DiCesare are for embracing my story, as it were his own. And giving it the fine-tuning in editing that it needed to shine.

I would also like to acknowledge Donna Davies for her hour's of advise as well as shaping me to be a better author, she is my mentor/guru of all thing's Halloween.

I guess I owe them monogrammed straight jackets for driving them crazy this year… But I love them for without them I could not have done this.

INTRODUCTION

I'm an independent paranormal investigator. I guess you can say I have always had a deep interest in the area of the paranormal, and as far back as I can recall.

What exactly is the paranormal? According to *Webster's Online Dictionary*, the first use of the word was noted back in 1920. And its meaning goes well before and beyond 1920; before the beginning of recorded time: strange events, abilities, etc. that cannot be explained by what is known about nature and the world that surrounds us.

For me, the paranormal is the continual existence of one's spirit - beyond life and physical death as we know it - and it's interaction with the living in everyday life. What matters is in what way we choose to accept this possibility, if we so choose to believe. Will you turn away from what you are unsure of as so many do? Or will you allow yourself to open up your mind, body and spirit and begin to scratch the surface for understanding of the 'unseen' and 'unheard'? A word of caution: My experience has taught me this: once you believe and begin to experience, you cannot walk away!

What solidified my decision to investigate the unseen, for the things that go bump in the night? The answers are contained within this book, but let me entice you with this: for five years my family and I lived in a house with some truly powerful spirits! But that their existence is only a part of this uncanny story. Just as importantly, it would take me many years to understand that not only were these spirits were very real, and the 'things' I had seen and heard real, but that a person's response to them was just as important.

I decided not to speak about my experiences as a young adult, as things of this nature were quite simply frowned upon. However, as many with experiences similar to me (although my story is quite unique) have come to realize, in recent years it has become more acceptable to hear, talk about and interact with what we call 'the paranormal'.

The events certainly took their toll on me, until I finally decided that I needed to embrace them, and the experience as a whole, 'full on'. To understand that there is something more than this physical life after we leave our bodies is very comforting. I ask that you join me as I share with you the all too real events of my paranormal experience.

Enjoy the journey!

THE HOME

The house was built in colonial style: boxy and white with a sorrowful face. Its pillars held up its cage of the damned. Slate and cement steps led up to the battleship gray porch. There was a white door with a diamond-shaped cut out window and mail slot as well as another wooden door with a large glass window adorned with sheer white curtains that 'greeted' any visitor. Every door within the home had the original glass door knobs.

The home contained a side room with a tiny entrance to hang wet raincoats or muddy boots and a large floor to ceiling built-in bookcase. The living room was big, a perfect square, with two pocket doors that pulled out and could 'close off' the living room from the dining room.

Off the dining room was a bedroom, which soon became my brother's room. In his room there was an adjoining door that led directly into another bedroom. This bedroom was, at first, was my room. It would later become my father's room after he had his two heart attacks. From the dining room doorway you were led down a very long foyer - I believe that this is commonly referred to as 'railroad' style.

My father's original bedroom, and the bathroom, had faux-marble wallpaper that I grew to hate because when in the bathroom I swear I could see the faces of tortured souls carved out of the patterns in it. Of course, I rationalized that away as I knew our mind's eye can make a habit of distorting things like that!

Next to the bathroom was my sister's bedroom - which I would later move into after my dad took over my room, as I mentioned previously.

At the end of the foyer was a linen closet where my mother would keep all of our bedding and towels. Off to the right side of the foyer was the kitchen, which was small but served its purpose as kitchens go. The kitchen's pantry had a window, which looked out over the back entrance, the cellar and the yard. Finally, the large wooden door to the back of the house had a glass window with a thick Venetian blind hooked to it.

1

I used to dread going into that small hallway that led to the yard because I would have to pass by the cellar door. The old steps were narrow, and there were what seemed to be over twenty steps to the bottom! I loathed going down there at any cost, even when my mother would have permission to use the washer and dryer, when once in a blue moon when the landlord had felt generous. Even at that young age, I always felt like something was chained to the floor, and looking at us. As crazy as it sounds to the rational mind, that remains the best image that I can provide to describe what I felt when I was down there.

The yard was somewhat large: one square section covered with grass and concrete. On the property was the original garage where the landlord and his hunting buddies would often hang dead deer upside down in order to 'cure' them. I detested playing in the yard when he did this. Through the large, thin glass windows of the garage I could see easily the dry staring eyes of the deer and their flesh-filled gutted open stomachs as they swung slowly – almost methodically – from the hooks that held them.

The entire home seemed to have an electric vibration that pulsated from somewhere within, as though some primal heartbeat was pumping out the blood of the soul-less into every crack in, and creak of, the floors.

HENRY

Henry was quite beyond his years, being that he was only nineteen. He kept to himself as much as he could with the exception of going into town to pick up his parcel deliveries. He would write to his mum in Manchester, England during the two years that he lived in the house. He eventually began to feel that the home he was currently residing in had some life force of its own. While never getting too detailed about the actual events that transpired, each letter that was sent back home became stranger and stranger. It was as if he was becoming delusional. Eventually his family would stop receiving correspondence from Henry altogether.

In years that would follow it seems that only those who were strong in faith would remain alive, and blessed be to those who still have some shred of sanity remaining in order to tell the tale.

The house remained empty thereafter, and the sun – as it always does – rose and set for almost two decades, before realtors slipped a key into the front door. Through the muted, dusty drapes that adorned the tall, wide windows, you could see the dust particles that streamed through the sun-lit kissed worn floors with your eyes. And there seemed to be some unseen force, a darkness that loomed from inside, and a quiet angry vibration that would quickly turn away even the happiest of potential homebuyers. As couples excitedly walked through the rooms, they would suddenly begin to argue and bicker as feelings of apprehension grew.

The local carpenters union went through workers like facial tissues on a cold, winter's day. During renovations to the home, it was reported that carpenters began to argue and blame one another for stealing each other's tools. Their electrical tools would disappear and then turn up in different by locations 'by themselves'. Soon neither contractors nor carpenters wanted to work there, much less to put in the overtime that was required in order to finish the job. These happenings caused many workmen to walk off the premises, which delayed the home being properly listed on the real estate market. Most people did not want to stay there for any length of time.

But the work still needed to be done, as it had been more than thirty years since the home had residents living within its walls. The structure had long stood vacant amongst a steadily growing, rising neighborhood. When the repairs were finally completed, the realtors placed a "For Sale" sign in front of the home in hopes of a quick sale.

Finally, in the mid-1940s, the Valeria family purchased the home on Lee Avenue. The shack of a home that Mr. Valeria and his family moved from was now becoming too unsafe and drafty for his family, so he set out to find a proper home to take better care of his wife and children. Mr. Anthony Valeria Sr. – as would any decent father – wanted to provide his wife, Sabrina, and three children (two daughter's Millicent and Graciella, and son Anthony Jr.) with a home.

But the pressures on Mr. Valeria were greater than most knew as his wife Sabrina was very ill, and in need of as much bed rest as possible. Her doctors had informed Mr. Valeria that his still youthful wife did not have much time left, as an incurable blood disorder was taking its toll on her small-framed body. Anthony Sr. tried to fight against this certain helplessness, placing Sabrina's and his fate into the hands of his faith.

He made a trip down to a church on the same avenue, an avenue that was now becoming more and more populated, lined with many family-owned stores. He quietly let himself into the church and knelt down onto his knees in front of the statue of the Virgin Mary. He began to shake and cry as he pleading with Mother Mary' and the heavens to reverse his beloved wife's condition. As he prayed the large door to the church blew open, smacking into the wall with great force and aloud noise. The very faithful Anthony Valeria was both stunned and frightened. Quickly making the Catholic sign of the cross, he pulled himself into an upright position. Fearing that it was an ill omen, he hurried down the aisle, the urgency to return home overcoming him.

As he began his hurried run up the block to check on his spouse his legs grew heavy, as if weights were tied to his feet, preventing him from running as fast as he suddenly felt that he needed to.

The children had been outside when they had heard the distinct sound of a chair falling over. All three of them ran inside, startled by what they discovered, screaming, "No mama! No mama! No mama!"

Anthony arrived home only to find his children wailing and crying as they gazed upon their mother's limp body.

"Go outside and let your mother rest," Anthony—perhaps out of habit—commanded the children.

Sabrina had waited until she was alone to slide a chair in the center of the pocket doors that led into the dining room. Using a bed sheet to secure around her neck, she had hung herself.

Anthony would find his wife's note on her bedside table:

"My darling family I love you but I am in too much pain. Forgive me."

THE LEASE

It was fall of 74', and after many long hours of apartment hunting, my mom and dad reached the last one on the list and decided that it was affordable. They called Mr. Valeria, the owner of the home, to advise him they decided to take the apartment if it was still available.

Mr. Valeria answered quickly, "Yes, yes, come right over!"

My parents loaded up the family car with my brother, sister and I to go sign the lease. I recall clearly being both hungry and tired when we went. Since I was just six years old I probably had the attention span of a flea. I can tell you that I recall being bored out of my mind by the whole process. I just wanted to just go home! My brother attempted to occupy me by doing some card tricks that he learned from a *K-Tel* magic kit that he had received for his birthday.

My mom and dad walked up to the front door, and the three of us filed behind them like small ducklings. When dad rang the bell it sounded like an old time telephone ringing. After a few moments, we heard footsteps beyond the door, we knew someone was about to let us in.

As the door pulled open, a small-framed man in his mid-fifties appeared in the place it had been. He was balding with dark eyes and was wearing a V-necked white T-shirt, and a pair of pleated brown slacks. A Saint Christopher medal hung around his neck. He offered his hand for my dad to shake.

My dad said, "I'm George, this is my wife Margie and these are our kids."

"I'm Tony Valeria Jr." He gestured for us to come in to take a look at the apartment. My mother bent down to me and whispered, "Don't touch anything," then instructed my brother and sister to keep an eye on me while we were there.

The Nigel family that was moving out still inhabited the apartment in this converted two-family home. It was coincidentally a family of five; however they had *two* sons and *one* daughter. The current owner noticed this and brought up that he too was one of three siblings and that his two

7

sisters live up on the second floor. Immediately we all saw the similar "family of five" pattern that had developed. Tony Valeria mentioned, "It would be nice if you met the current family when you sign the lease, so that if you have any questions, now would be a perfect time to ask."

The Nigel family and Mr. Valeria sat down with my family and I at the dining room table to review the lease and inform us what was – and was not – included in the rental agreement.

I remember intently eying the Italian pastries that were displayed in the middle of the table on an organized cookie platter. I wanted a pastry so bad, eating one of those might make the trip a worthwhile one for me. Since I was too shy to ask Mr. Valeria, I carefully tugged on my mom's shirtsleeve until she looked down. "What's wrong?"

I asked: "Can I have a pastry?"

"Would it be alright if my daughter had a pastry?" my mom questioned the man.

He nodded and smiled. "Of course my dear, help yourself."

Music to my ears! I reached for the *petit four*, which is still my favorite!

By this time the autumn sun had been down for a good hour. It was slightly after 8:00pm and day had transitioned into a rather dark and starless night. As our two families chatted about the apartment, their daughter, Robin Nigel, asked me, "Do you want to see your new room?"

I said, "Sure!" and jumped up and followed her.

The room had been artistically painted; the walls were adorned with red and white roses judiciously brushed on, so as to look like wallpaper. Robin had a small piano in her room and she asked if I wanted to learn how to play. I of course said, "YES!"

We sat on the piano bench side by side. She then began by showing me the keys, and I did my best to copy exactly what she did with her fingers. 'This was wonderful' I thought to myself. I was laughing, and just as Robin had finished saying that I was playing very well, the glass lamp on Robin's nightstand slid across the wooden table top and fell onto the floor, shattering into too many pieces to count! As Robin scrambled into the darkness to turn on the ceiling light fixture, she exclaimed: "Don't worry, this always happens."

My mother immediately came running into the room, thinking that it was me who had broken the lamp.

"Don't worry, it was neither of us," said Robin without alarm.

Mrs. Nigel came into the room with a dustpan, looking at Robin rather nervously. Robin smiled and slowly shook her head, as if she were saying "No" to her mom. My mother then took me by the hand and led me out of Robin's bedroom.

I could always tell when my dad was angry. He had this weird expression where his eyes would roll around as if to say "NOW WHAT?!" He would then throw his hands 'up to God', lower his voice an octave, and call out whoever's name he felt had caused the situation. In this case it was a loud and clear: "DONNA!"

Like my mother had, he immediately assumed that I broke something on our first visit, this when a good impression was so very important. My mom tried to reassure my dad that it wasn't me this time. As everyone was already on their feet in an attempt to discover what had actually happened in the room, Tony Valeria said in a half-joking way: "We should wrap this meeting up before something else breaks." He then politely laughed at his own joke as he rocked in his shoes at what he considered his own cleverness.

My parents signed on the 'dotted line' and it was agreed that we would all move in on Tuesday, October 1st, 1974. My dad and Mr. Valeria shook hands after signing the lease, and then we all piled back into the old white car. Once we got back onto the car my mother looked over the front seat at me and asked, "So what really happened in that room that a lamp broke?"

I said, "Mommy, we were at the piano. I was learning how to play *Mary Had a Little Lamb* and the lamp flew off the night table. Robin said it always happens."

My father replied, "They probably have mice. We can buy traps when we move in."

There was an odd silence for the remainder of the ride home. I can't recall either my brother or sister speaking a single word. A sudden, unexplainable, tension had taken over every one of us.

THE FIRST NIGHT

The night before we were set to actually move in, my mother received the keys from Tony Valeria so that she would be able to clean up ahead of the move. Alone, she drove herself over to the new apartment. Entering the home with her cleaning supplies in hand, the first thing she did was turn on the lights in every room, while opening all the windows to air out the apartment. After she set her thermal coffee container on the stovetop, she tied her hair back off of her face with a red and white bandanna and slipped some rubber gloves onto her hands in order to scrub the bathtub. While she was bent over the tub scrubbing she heard a door open in the house.

"Hello?" she called out.

No one answered her, so she assumed it was a door being blown open from the wind. She started scrubbing the tub once again as she sang aloud to herself "You Are My Sunshine" as she often sang while doing housework. Moments later, the faint sound of footsteps could then be heard coming from the next room. Since there was no furniture in the apartment yet, every sound was amplified. This time she stopped her work, pulling the rubber gloves off her hands.

Cautiously, she maneuvered herself down the short foyer and tip–toed over to where she thought she heard the footsteps. She saw nothing, waited a moment, and heard no other sounds. After making the sign of the cross, my mother said a prayer and proceeded back to the kitchen where she had placed her thermal container of coffee.

"Where is my coffee?" she asked, puzzled because she knew very well she placed it on the stovetop.

She was unable to call anyone as the phone was off and not due to be turned on until the following morning. At that time, back in 1974, there were no cell phones to be had. She decided instead to run to the landlord's apartment. A she reached his door she rang the buzzer to see if anyone had come downstairs and removed her coffee container. Perhaps it was Tony or one of his sisters, she reasoned to herself. No one came to the door. From the outside looking in she could not see any lights on, the apartment was dark.

"They must have gone out after they gave me the keys," she said to herself.

With no answers, my mother returned to the apartment to finish the necessary cleaning before the following day's big move. Yet she was still shaken by the evening's unexplained events, and as she moved quietly through the apartment she kept a watchful eye out for her thermal coffee container. Grabbing the aluminum stepladder she headed for what was soon to be my sister's bedroom. As she stepped up onto the ladder (while holding up a pair of drapes) and placed the curtain rod onto the hooks: "BANG!"

At that precise moment the bedroom door, which was directly behind her, slammed shut jarring her to the point where she almost fell backwards off of the ladder. Her hands were trembling uncontrollably.

"I'm leaving!" she announced.

Grabbing her jacket, handbag and car keys, she fled the apartment with no concern as to whether or not she had switched off the lights or locked the doors before she did so.

As she drove home her hands were still trembling. "Our Father who art in Heaven hallowed by thy name..." she prayed over and over until she had returned to our current apartment.

She did not know how to explain to her husband, much less her children, what had happened in the new place. My father never expressed any belief in "ghosts" so he typically shrugged off such stories as 'bullshit'. She left him alone to continue his sleep on the couch. My mom obviously felt that I was too young at that time to comprehend, so she decided to keep the events of that night from me for many, many, years.

Yet my older sister and my brother (who were fourteen and fifteen years old at that time) were acutely aware that *something* was wrong with our mother. My sister put the kettle on for some tea and then she and my brother sat down next to my mom.

After a few anxious moments, my mother confided in them the details of her frightening experience: "I really don't know what to do Doreen. I know that I am not going crazy. I know what I heard. I know what I felt. I felt as if I was being 'watched' and that whatever it was — or whoever it was — does not want us there. But it's too late.

We have to move there. There is no time left to stay here. We already signed the damned lease!"

As might be expected, my sister Doreen initially looked at her in disbelief. It was not that she didn't believe my mother had experienced something, but the whole scenario made little sense to her. After all, we had never lived there and no one in the home had known who we were, so why would this be happening to *us*?

My brother had been sitting there quietly, listening. Like my dad in some ways, he would normally try to find a logical, scientific reason for when an 'unusual' thing took place. He said, "Mom, it will be fine. I really think you are overreacting and it was probably nothing more than an open window that caused this to happen."

Looking back it was obvious that he simply wanted my mom to feel at ease with what she went through. On the other hand, my sister Doreen – having seen and heard the intensity of my mom's recollection of the events – came to the considered conclusion that something supernatural *had* occurred. She believed.

In my mother's mind, whatever it was that had been in those rooms with her was definitely not of this world! The fright that she had so personally experienced that evening made it increasingly difficult for her to fall sleep. But as the hours slowly passed, exhaustion eventually overtook her. She fell into a deep slumber with her still warm Rosary beads clenched securely in her hands.

MOVING DAY

My mom woke early the following morning, around 3 a.m. Perhaps her recent memories forced her awake at that early hour. She put the coffee up, went into the bathroom to splash her face and then got dressed. Her mind continued to race with thoughts about the experience that she had at the new apartment, but she also knew she had to somehow get beyond these dread feelings and ignore whatever it was. She swept up and cleaned the apartment that we were moving from, and packed up some last minute items to bring over to the new place.

One by one the rest of my family woke up, and we started to assemble our belongings together. We were informed that the moving truck would be arriving any minute so we had to hurry. My dad was typically a little grumpy during the morning hours. This morning was no exception to the rule. And if my mother had thought for a moment to share her experience from the night before, his current mood dissolved that thought immediately! As the moving van pulled up, we all brought our boxes, bags etc. to the front of the apartment in order to make it easier for the moving men to retrieve them and bring them to the truck.

As the morning dragged on, my brother and I started to 'clown around' a bit. I started to belly laugh and run around, all the while getting perhaps just a little too hyper! In my defense though, I probably acted like any six year old would when 'hopped up' on sugary soda during the morning of our big family move. My dad snapped "God Dammit! Donna knock "yer" shit off already!"

My brother saved me: "Sorry, dad, it was me. I was joking around with Donna. Don't yell at her." I retreated to a corner and became quiet..

THE ARTIST
(ALSO KNOW AS, HENRY MUND)

Once in our new home, my brother began going through his closet in order to clean and organize it. As he did so, a poster tube that had been resting on the very top shelf, fell on his head. It was fully covered in dust and looked as though it hadn't been moved in decades.

"Mom!" he called as he walked hurriedly with the object into the dining room.

"Oh. What is that?" she asked, as she came walking in from the direction of the living room, where she had been cleaning.

Without fail my sister and I trailed behind her to see why he seemed so excited. He held up the poster tube. To my mind it was some type of long-hidden treasure, now discovered! My brother removed the end cap, peeked in, and viewed the rolled up parchment type paper that was yellowed around the edges. Carefully, he slid the large rolled document out of protective tube. Once free of its casing, we unrolled it across the dining room table with each of us holding a corner so it would not roll back up. We studied the 'poster' with interest as the realization dawned on us: it was an architectural blueprint of the very house we now lived in. The name of the designer was listed on the document: Henry Mund. The year as well: 1910. To me it was amazing that over the years no other tenant living appeared to have located it.

How was it possible that no one had secured this document? Over the ensuing years I have wondered, was it *meant* to be seen by us? Was Henry Mund one of the spirits that would, as time moved forward, created the supernatural activities that would plague us?

My brother decided to research this topic some more. He traveled down to City Hall with our mother later that afternoon and asked, "May I see the prints you have on file for the house?" as he provided the address.

Since most construction documents are considered to be 'public domain' you can often obtain copies of them at little cost. A particularly odd fact emerged though. Henry Mund, according to more than a few older neighbors who heard the stories from their parents, had moved into the home while it was still an un-insulated farmhouse. There was seemingly no way that he could have designed the home. He was a young man of just nineteen when he traveled 'across the pond' to live and work in America.

So what exactly was happening here? Was this some elaborate hoax? Perhaps Mund had constructed a blueprint of what he *thought* should have been? Or was there an underlying secret embedded within this drawing?

We never did find out. When we asked Mr. Valeria he denied having any knowledge of the print that sat in the closet for decades. Perhaps he spoke the truth. But it stands to reason that if you live in a house long enough you begin to learn all its' secrets over time.

As a naturally inquisitive – sometimes maudlin – child, I thought to myself, what if I started to try to communicate with this Henry Mund?

My mother had gone to take a bath, my brother and sister were out with their friends and my dad had left the house to get a newspaper. To this day I do not know what possessed me to sit on that couch, to just start talking aloud to this 'Henry' person who was quite possibly haunting our home.

I said: "Hello, Henry. I am Donna. Why are you here? Are you sad? Do you want to be my friend?"

At that point I heard the bathroom door open, "Who are you speaking to?"

"Nobody, mommy! I was just playing with Sammy."

Sammy was a Chihuahua that we had adopted from a dying woman in Haverstraw, New York some time before.

Later that day I had a strong urge to draw. I could not draw well back then and to this day I still can't draw to save my life, but what child doesn't enjoy coloring and drawing? It wasn't much. Just stick people, a stick dog and a sick and sad looking pink sun. My sister came home later that day. She had been standing at the kitchen sink washing the dishes. I decided that I wanted to show my sister the picture that I drew. She is very artistic and I wanted her approval on my 'stick figure' work of art.

"Doreen! Doreen! I have a picture I want to show you!"

She smiled and said, "Okay."

I picked up the construction paper with the stick people drawn on it. As I held it up to show her, it felt as if a football player ran into me and knocked me into the kitchen wall, throwing me approximately four feet back and off of my feet. My sister screamed and ran over to me.

The wind had been knocked out of my lungs. I was frightened and it was difficult to breathe. Doreen lifted me to my feet and carried me to the bedroom. I was shaking and crying. I could not understand what had just happened to me.

Once in the room, she said it was the strangest looking thing she had ever seen. She said that it looked as if I someone had run into, slightly lifted, and then slammed me into the wall. The only problem with her

18

analysis was that no one was there!

Doreen screamed, "Mom!"

My mother had been outside checking the mailbox.

The attack had left my back bruised, and my tailbone was in pain from the way that I had fallen on the floor. I recall being quite sore for almost two weeks after the incident. I wondered to myself if Henry Mund had been responding to the poor quality of my artwork. Or perhaps the entity knew that I was trying to communicate with it, and not wanting me to do so, responded in this violent way?

I had heard from someone that young children such as I could communicate with spirits a little easier than adults could; that the 'channels' are clearer and spirits were more open to receiving information from the young, the innocent. So even though being thrown against the wall scared the hell out of me, I still wanted to pursue communicating with Mr. Mund, or whatever spirits were in the home. I wanted to know why they were doing what they were doing us.

Obviously, I had no clear idea how to expect – or control – what came next. Some 'door', some 'portal' of communication seemed to be wedged open, causing these terrible things to happen. But I was so young and inexperienced that I did not know how to shut it down even if I had wanted to. If you have seen the move The Exorcist then you will remember what Captain Howdy did to little Reagan right? Taking spiritual matters into your own hands should never be taken lightly. EVER. This is an awfully big life lesson.

RING—AROUND—THE—ROSY

I was excited to have my own room, even though I had a connecting door that led to my brother's bedroom. I admit I was a bit scared to be in this room after the incident at the lease signing. The walls were painted a bloody red and there were pink roses stenciled all over it. My closet door had been painted so many times that it would no longer shut completely. I dreaded that the closet would not shut, especially at night when I went to sleep. I also had a habit of falling out of bed so she always placed a safety rail on the side of the bed. At times I would sleepwalk and my mom would find me curled up on the floor in the corner of the bedroom.

My mom had set up my twin bed with fresh bedding and new pillows, and I placed one of my favorite dolls in the center of the freshly made bed. Even though it was old, I loved it. It had been handed down to me from when my sister who had it since she herself was a baby. The doll had blinking eyelids and some of her hair was lopped off from playing too many sessions of 'beauty parlor' over the years.

"Time to take your bath now, Donna," my mom said as she hung the rest of my clothes up in the closet. The bathroom was the next room over and she was able to keep and ear open for me. She would call out every few minutes, "Donna, you alright?" I would answer, "Yeah ma" … [Splash! Splash! Splash!]

The phone rang. My mom stopped what she was doing and walked to the rotary phone which was hung on a wall phone in the kitchen. As I finished up in the tub I heard my mom say, "Hi Mamma." It was my grandmother. I wrapped a towel around me and walked into my bedroom to finish drying off and get dressed. My doll was missing. I had just placed her there minutes ago. I ran into the kitchen to discover that my mom was still on the phone talking with my grandmother. She was facing the window as she spoke.

"Ma," I said.

"Wait a minute Donna"

"Ma! Where did my doll go? I put her on my bed."

"Mama I have to call you back, Donna needs me."

I walked with her into the bedroom and the doll was on the bed right where I had originally placed her.

"She was there all the time," my mother said. But I saw that she was missing when I went in there following my bath.

"Just ignore it," mom said.

I got changed for bed. I overheard my mother whisper to my brother, Larry. "Did you mess around with Donna's doll?"

"No Ma!" Larry assured her. "I am setting up my desk working on homework."

She mumbled to herself, "I don't understand what she was talking about."

I was now in bed as my bedtime usually fell between 8:30 to 9 p.m. I waited for my Mom to come in and say goodnight. After doing so, as she went to leave the room, she turned the light off.

"Can you leave the light on?" I asked.

"Larry is still up in the next room, the foyer light is on. You don't need your light on Donna, be a big girl."

So she shut the light out.

I hated the dark as a child. As I felt myself start to drift off into a light sleep, I heard a little girl's voice. I felt the blood rush out of my head and my eyes sprung open. The voice, emanating from my bedroom closet, began singing "Ring-Around-The-Rosy a Pocket Full of Posey's, Ashes, Ashes, we all fall down."

"Ma! Ma! Maaaaaaaaa!"

I froze! I couldn't move as I was paralyzed by fear. I heard my brother open the connecting door and my mom shuffled up the foyer from living room. "What is wrong?"

The singing had stopped. I told both my brother and my mother what I had heard. My brother decided to open the closet door all the way. "There is nothing there Donna. How much sugar did you eat today?" my brother said in a tired and sarcastic tone rolling his eyes. "I think it's your imagination Donna."

"Please, please, can I sleep in the living room on the couch?"

"No you can't get into that habit. I'll leave your room light on until you fall asleep," said my mother.

I can remember lying there ... alone ... for what seemed an eternity just staring at the closet door. In my mind I can still see the manner in which the foyer hall light shined through my room highlighting the opening of the closet. I wrapped my arms around my pillow tightly – as if a simple bed pillow would save me – and I eventually drifted off to sleep. The next thing I remember was the sun was coming up and my mom walking into my room to wake me for school.

"Can I stay home today? I don't feel good."

"No. Why don't you go to school and see how you feel. If you are still not feeling well by lunchtime I will pick you up."

"Did you hear that little girl again?" she asked cautiously.

"No mom, I did not, but she was there," I insisted. "I don't like my room. Can I sleep in Doreen's room from now on?" "Donna you have your own room now."

THE DEAD BOY'S ROOM

My dad had suffered a heart attack, and he was recovering from open-heart surgery at home. My mother decided to move me into my sister's bedroom, to share it with her. Mom thought giving my dad his own room would be better for him to recuperate

My sister's room was the last bedroom off the hallway. I remember the walls being bright blue to match the sky. They were adorned with rock n' roll posters and famous leading men of the 1970s. Looking back I feel bad that my sister had to give up her privacy and share her room with her sister who was nine years younger. I was still playing with stuffed animals and dolls. But she was always good to me and never made me feel unwelcome. I admired her clothes and shoes and constantly begged her to paint my fingernails, but my mother forbade make-up or nail polish on me (unless it was for Halloween or a school play).

One night after we both went to bed – it must have been between three and four in the morning – I awoke out of a deep sleep. I thought that I had heard someone enter the bedroom. The light from the foyer illuminated our room, so I was able to see a little bit. I saw no one enter the room. Before I could say anything, from the left side of the bed, the side I slept on, I heard a male voice say, "Hello."

It was a deep, raspy male voice. I started to scream. I closed my eyes because I was afraid to see who or what was talking to me.

Before I could do anything else what happened next was even more frightening. Our window blinds on the window directly in front of the bed started to flare out towards our bed as if something were trying to bust through the window. My sister woke up and she started to scream as well. My mother and brother heard us from down the hallway and quickly ran over to us. They flipped on the light switch and the aluminum blinds were mangled and lying on the floor. It looked as if someone wrestled with them.

"I woke up and heard a man's voice say hello to me then the blinds went nuts!" I cried.

My brother, playing detective, looked over to the direction the blinds was bent from.

"It looks like something has bent the aluminum from the outside in."

We could not go back to sleep after this happened. We piled into the living room and watched TV until the sun rose over the horizon. We all had school the next morning and we dragged our feet from exhaustion behind us. Our attention span that day was hindered to say the least.

My mother was home that day caring for my dad, he had gone to my old room to take a nap. As my mom dusted the furniture, the doorbell rang. She looked through the curtains and noticed two police officers standing by the door. Her eyes were wide with worry as she opened the door.

"Can I help you?" she asked nervously.

One the officers asked, "Do you have a son named Larry?"

She began to feel a bit unsteady, and her heart started to race. She stumbled on the word, "Yes."

They said, "Mam, your son Larry was found this morning dead at the Yonkers Motor Inn from a heroin over dose."

My mother fell to her knees and howled and cried out, "Noooo! God, no!"

My father awoke from all of the commotion. He walked out to the living room where the officers were trying to console my mother.

"What is going on? What happened?"

One of the officers said, "Are you Mr. Nigel?"

"No, why?" said my father.

"What is your last name?" said the officer.

My father snapped "Parish. Why? What is this about?"

"Isn't your son Larry Nigel?"

Confused my mother looked up and said, "What? Our son is Larry Parish. Larry Nigel was the boy who used to live here. His family moved to Florida when they moved out a few weeks ago."

It was a huge mistake. The Yonkers Police Department had never asked my mother what her name was from the beginning of the conversation. An even stranger coincidence that my brother had the same first name and was the same age of Larry Nigel who just moved out weeks before.

That evening, Mr. Valeria came downstairs to discuss the death of Larry Nigel. He sat down in my dad's chair (we called it the Archie Bunker chair). No one was allowed to sit in that chair except for my dad. He would read his newspapers and watch the news on TV in it. My mom had a nervous look on her face because Tony just plopped down in the chair. My dad was expressionless. My mother offered coffee before they sat down to talk about what had happened.

Tony politely declined, "No, thank you Margie." He had mentioned that Larry Nigel had gotten involved with the wrong crowd, left school, and started doing drugs. He actually was stealing from his own parents.

Apparently when the Nigels moved out of this apartment to move to Florida, they had begged him to go with them and to get help at a rehab facility. But he decided to run out before they moved, and they had no idea where he had gone. So when the police found his body, this was his last known address.

We discovered that Larry Nigel died in the middle of the night, the same night we had that incident occur in our room. And Mr. Valeria informed us that the room in the back (my sister's bedroom in which I now shared) was in fact Larry Nigel's bedroom. Could it be that he thought that he was coming home and just going about his normal everyday routine? I wondered if he had joined the rest of the inventory of lost souls that inhabited the Lee Avenue Home?

Night after night, following the overdose of Larry Nigel, we noticed increased activity in our room. Activity that just could not be explained with a simple "must have been a breeze" or "perhaps your overtired and you are talking yourself into seeing and hearing these things." It became clear that his recent death had brought more energy to the home, leading to amplified poltergeist activity.

One late night my sister awoke because she heard the closet door squeak open slowly. She was frozen with fear, and couldn't even scream. She didn't want to wake me because she didn't want me to be even more afraid of the room. Her eyes focused on the closet door as she remained paralyzed with fright. Then there it was: a small dark mass gliding along the floor that took the shape of some animal. When it looked up at her she noticed the eyes were like a raccoon, yet its face was shaped into almost human features and it bared its teeth like a psychotic person smiling. She suspects she passed out from fright when it smiled at her as she could not remember anything beyond that. The following day she explained this incident to my mother.

My mother waited until all of us were out of the house when she broke out her *Bible* and Holy Water. She went through each and every room dousing the carpets and floors, beds and anywhere we would sit, lie down or walk. "Our Father who art in Heaven hallowed by thy name..." she recited over and over again. "Please protect us in the name of Jesus Christ." She had a strong faith but there are times that no matter how strong your faith is, Evil plays with your mind and tugs at your faith, dismantling it piece by piece until your sanity hangs by a few shredded threads..

PYRAMID OF CHAIRS

It was a school holiday, a teachers' meeting day, so we had the day off from school. I recall that there was snow outside and that it was too cold to go out and play with my friends. My sister had decided to take out her sketchpad and draw her fashion designs. My brother was sleeping late and my mom was at the supermarket picking up dinner for that night.

I turned on our kitchen radio and listened to WABC radio. I opened up my Barbie dollhouse on the kitchen table. It started out like any other seemingly normal morning. My dad was out at a doctor's appointment for a medical check-up. I also recall begging my sister to make pancakes. I loved the way she made them. She didn't cook them all the way through so that the insides were almost like raw cookie dough. My mother did not want me to then raw for fear that I might get sick. I would eat them anyway, and I never got sick!

Larry's bedroom was directly off the dining room. His door was shut as, the kitchen door too, so that the music on the radio would not disturb him as he was sleeping. My sister and I were talking as she sketched gowns and shoes on her pad. I remember breaking into fits of giggling about something my sister had said.

Then we heard my brother yelling in a panic, "What the fuck? What did you do to me?"

We and also heard sounds as if he was struggling to get out of his bedroom. He came running into the kitchen with a petrified look on his face and out of breath.

"I had to run through the other room! Why did you do that to me?" he asked, looking back and forth at each my sister and I.

We had no idea what he was talking about.

"You didn't do that to me?" he asked skeptically.

Again we both looked confused at him, but now we were both becoming scared and worried.

"What Larry? What is wrong? What happened?" we asked. "Come with me, and I will show you!"

We followed him into the dining room, which faced his room. We stood there staring in utter disbelief. We gasped and covered our mouths with our hands. All of the dining room chairs, including the captains' chairs, were piled in a pyramid fashion, neatly stacked up against my brother's door!

He really thought *we* did that in order to have some fun with him, but we honestly had no idea that this had even taken place. Perhaps just as odd was the fact that neither of us ever heard any of the chairs moving the entire time we were in the kitchen. That image will remain in my brain as long as I live. This entity clearly loved screwing with our minds!

We decided to leave the chairs in the fashion we found them, so that we could show then to our mom when she got back from the supermarket. We sat in the living room together and kept popping up like prairie dogs looking out the window every time we heard a car pull up. Finally she drove up and we ran out to her to grab the bags and also prepare her for what happened.

She walked slowly into the entranceway of the living room as we all shuffled behind her. As we reached the threshold of the dining room, the chair that was balanced on top of the pyramid suddenly tipped forward, in our direction. The wood of the chair was so old that the frame of the chair came apart. We all just jumped and screamed and looked at each other.

"Please don't tell your father."

She knew that he would get upset knowing we couldn't afford to move at this time. We all helped to put the groceries away. My mom prepared lunch and suggested we eat on the porch just to get out of the apartment for a few minutes.

Every day there seemed to be a new and frightening experience. I am only sorry we never had a camera or video camera to record it so that we could show everyone. All we have are the battle scars from Lee Avenue.

PRAYERS AND HOLY WATER

As each day unfolded it came with a new experience for every family member. It seemed as if this entity (or entities) that cohabitated with my family tried to make himself (or herself) known in some form or another. Our mother was a devout Catholic and her salvation came in the form of a rosary, a Bible, Holy Water and a prayer. But tragically enough it seemed as if with every psalm my mother spoke, things elevated to a new level of malevolence.

As my mother doused the floors, beds and closets with Holy Water she recited, "Our Father, which art in heaven, Hallowed be thy Name. Thy Kingdom come, Thy will be done in earth, as it is in heaven. Give us this day our daily bread, and forgive us our trespasses, as we forgive those that trespass against us. And lead us not into temptation, but deliver us from evil. For thine is the kingdom, and the power, and the glory, forever and ever. Amen."

As she recited this prayer over and over, the room's temperature would drop like we were the middle of a wasteland in a dead and icy winter. Things would seem quiet and somber for a day or two after she sprinkled the Holy Water, but then they would eventually come back with vengeance, as though to let her know that they were *not* happy!

SPEAKING IN TONGUES

I woke up feeling sick. My mother allowed me to stay home from school this particular day and I had slept late. I remember hearing my brother and sister rush around in the madness of the morning. I could smell the coffee perking on the stovetop (I loved that smell early in the morning) and I could hear the 'pop' of the toaster.

"More burnt toast," my mother grumbled. "We must need a new toaster because it's been burning all the bread no matter what setting we put it on."

I looked across the room and our dog, Sammy, was still sleeping in his little dog bed. I loved that dog; I felt safe with him. It just felt as if he were watching over me. As long as he was in the room with me, and I could hear all the commotion going on in the kitchen, I felt secure.

After my brother and sister headed out the door to go to school, my mom started to clean and tidy up the place. I wandered out and took a seat at the kitchen table, made myself a cup of tea and some burnt toast. When I was finished, I went into the living room to keep my mother company as she dusted and vacuumed the living room. Sammy followed behind me, my little faithful companion. He 'plopped down' right in the center of the living room floor and watched my mother. I was standing next to her in the center of the living room just chatting away like I normally did at that age. Sammy's ears suddenly went back, and he sprung up to his feet. He faced my dad's chair, which no one was sitting (or so we thought). He started to bark and growl and would not take his stare off that chair. Within seconds, we heard a deep male voice speaking in what sounded like no other language I have ever heard before. Perhaps Latin, but what the hell did we know? My mother and I grabbed onto each other and screamed. Sammy yelped and ran behind the old large console television. We were too terrified to move past the chair to run to the kitchen where the telephone was. We were frozen with fear just like this thing, this entity, clearly wanted. It was deliberately trying to scare the shit out of us. And I will let you all in on a little secret: it succeeded!

My mother called my grandmother on the phone later that day and told her about all of the awful things that had been happening to the family in that home.

"Call the church," my grandmother suggested, "have a priest come over and bless it."

My mother walked down the block to our local parish. The parish priest was Father Gallagher. He dyed his hair a shoe-polish black and tended to flirt with the women that came to church. Personally, I never trusted or liked him.

"I will do no such thing," said Father Gallagher. "I refuse to come to your house and instead of a priest I suggest you see a psychologist!"

"Please, please, you must help me," my mother sobbed, begging him to help.

I sat in the rectory near her, playing with my magnetic game, Wooly Willy (you know the picture of the bald dude that you used magnetic shavings on to create a beard and hair).

"Please leave because there is nothing I can do for you."

My mother, feeling helpless and alone, took my hand and we reluctantly walked down the street back to the house. She would have to tell my brother and sister when they got back home. She tried to explain this to my dad but he became annoyed and sarcastic with her, actually insinuating that we were making it all up for attention.

We went to a library and some book stores to see if they had anything on the subject of 'hauntings'. There were a few books that seemed to have stories with similar situations to our own. While that made us feel less alone, there were no 'cures', no answers on how to make it leave. We would have to leave, but we had nowhere to go. Who could help us? Where do we turn? We were completely paralyzed.

My dad was still out on disability and he was receiving social security checks to help pay the rent and eat. Moving was not an option for us, so each day would unfold as a new experience. These experiences heightened our belief in the paranormal, while at the same time decreasing my faith in the Catholic Church for turning their back on us. My mother's faith, however, never teetered. It only grew stronger.!

EVIL CARICATURES

One day while my brother, my sister and I were at school, my mother started cleaning the house. She went into my brother's room to vacuum, dust and make the bed. It was then that she noticed demonic faces drawn (with a blue pen) on my brother's desktop where he sat to do his homework. The ink was still wet! These were awful faces, that almost looked like they were evil versions of our family. My mother waited until we came home from school then asked my brother about it.

"I don't know what you are talking about," he told my mother.

"Look at this," she pointed.

When she showed him his desk, you could have knocked him over with a feather. He immediately turned pale, and his knees buckled. In a trembling voice he said, "I swear I didn't do this!"

They both tried to remove the images with alcohol, and then painted over them with paint that my mom had found in the linen closet. It was an antique white colored paint. But the ink seemed to faintly bleed through no matter what they did. Seeing hints and outlines of these awful faces taunted and reminded all of us that 'it' wasn't leaving and that we were the intruders.

MARY HAD A LITTLE LAMB—INDEED

It was a sunny, crisp, spring afternoon. My mom was washing the curtains and drapes in the house to freshen up the place. She climbed the step stool to hang up the white cotton curtains, trimmed on the bottom with delicate eyelet lace, in our bedroom. We sat on the bed watching her and chatted away.

"When I'm done with the curtains I'm going to put the kettle up to make tea."

She stepped down off the stool and folded it up, tucked it under her arm and left the room. My sister reached into her nightstand drawer to get the book she was reading. She wanted to take it into the kitchen while we had our afternoon tea. I opened the closet door and asked her if I could wear her big red-wedged shoes around the house. I used to love to dress up in my sister's clothing. She had such a keen eye for fashion and still does to this day.

"Sure, just don't break your neck because mommy will kill me."

As I reached into the closet, which was oddly-shaped in that it was narrow, but went back about six or seven feet, I reached down to grab the shoes. I heard a little girl singing:

"Mary had a Little Lamb, Little Lamb" …then started to giggle in a playful way.

I froze.

My sister heard her, too. I started to scream, "Doreen, Doreen, Doreen!"

She ran over, grabbed me by the hand, and dragged me out of the room. I couldn't stop shaking. My sister and I ran into the kitchen and my mother spun around, with a frightened look. "What happened? Why are you shaking?"

We told her what we heard in the closet. And then it dawned on me: I remembered what happened the night we met the Nigel family who had lived here before. Their daughter Robin was teaching me how to play 'Mary

Had a Little Lamb' on her piano when the lamp flew off her nightstand.
This was no coincidence.

Either this was a little girl, or was pretending to be. Either way it was sick. I no longer wanted to go into the closets to get my clothes. I made my mom get them from then on. I also had to make sure the closet doors were shut tight at night and latched. I had my mom put a hook and eye latch on the outside to ensure it would not open. Yet, all this might have been done in vain. After all, if these beings could appear and disappear, sing aloud, draw pictures, move furniture, and speak in tongues, did I really think that a small Woolworth brand hook and eye latch would keep that closet shut at night? !

PUTRID ODORS AND PUDDLES

My family also noticed the apartment came with its own 'essence'. It was more than mold or moisture since we actually had none of those issues at all. The fact that these odors came out of nowhere, and then would leave just as quickly, left us reeling. The best description of this odor I can share was of damp farmland that animals had urinated and defecated on mixed with the smell of wet farm animal fur and wool. We would often find puddles of water and secretions of syrupy-like liquid in several spots of the house. My mother would clean them up and look for logical reasons behind these puddles. But we could not find the source.

One morning, as my mother, brother, sister and I sat at the kitchen table having breakfast, something frightening occurred. We were having tea and chatting with one another.

"Mom, can we stop at Cross County to go to Woolworths? I want to see if the Halloween costumes are out?"

She answered, "We'll see, hon. I have to make sure I am home in time to make dinner."

Out of nowhere a good-sized cup's worth of this fluid came down on my mother's head soaking it and leaving her breathless. This liquid was clear, but thick to the touch, almost like egg white consistency.

We all shouted and screamed. There is no way to explain what or how it happened. There were no leaks in the ceiling. My mother gasped and was in shock and frightened by this phenomena. She quickly jumped up and ran to the sink to rinse her hair. She was shaking and started to cry at this point. It was clear to her that this presence was evil, and that it was making it clear that it wanted us out of that house.

She washed her hair and prayed and shouted out commands such as, "May the powers of Christ compel you" much like in the movie "The Exorcist." My mother was desperate at this point and wanted her family safe once and for all. We also noticed there were these yellowish drops that would stain a newspaper we were reading, a letter we had been writing, or the homework we were working on. It was almost as if tears were dropping onto surfaces throughout our home. It was sorrowful, whatever this being inside the home was, filled with so much hate, anger and despair. We would often notice these yellow drops of liquid on my sister's drawings or my mother's shopping or 'to-do' lists. We tried to research what these yellowish puddles and stains could be and the closest thing we reasoned was ectoplasm. Many contemporary skeptics will state there is no such thing as ectoplasm, but if you lived for twenty-four hours in that house, I think that they would change their minds!

The theory on ectoplasm is that it is a spirit trying to materialize. Since we had no ceiling leaks and no other source where this syrupy fluid was apparently coming from, ectoplasm was the only answer at this point. Everything else was ruled out.

THE SHAPE

It was around ten in the evening. My dad and brother were asleep. Doreen was in the kitchen with my mother who was cleaning up the pots and pans from dinner. Mom went into another room and left my sister in the kitchen. As my sister sat there drawing, she noticed some movement by the entrance of the kitchen. My sister thought her eyes were playing tricks with her. In her peripheral vision she kept noticing some shape moving about by the entrance of the kitchen hiding and popping up and down by the refrigerator. She thought it was our mom at first playing around with her. Smiling and shaking her head thinking "Aha! Very funny, Ma!" She looked down at her sketchpad to continue to draw. Again she saw the movement. She looked up and saw, for lack of a better description, 'thing'. After she realized it was no one in the family, she felt the blood drain from her face and she became paralyzed with fear.

It was about five feet in height. It had long, dark, flowing hair. It was almost 'faceless'. As if the facial features were blurred out with an eraser. Doreen screamed! My mom unlatched the bathroom door and flew down the hallway making a mad dash for the kitchen.

"What's wrong, Doreen?" she asked in a breathless and nervous tone.

My sister was shaking, and frozen in fear in the corner of the kitchen. She was grabbing her face with both her hands like the painting "The Scream". Once my sister calmed down a bit she explained what she had seen to my mother.

"And then I thought it was you playing a joke on me."

This anomaly apparently knew when to strike and knew our weaknesses. It appeared to us when we were alone, trying to make us feel like we were going crazy. Another time she saw the shape when she was in the bathroom. Our bathroom's toilet was separated from the bathtub with a wall partition. So that if you were sitting 'doing your business' you would have to lean forward and to the left, to see the bathtub. While my sister was seated, she noticed something move near the wall partition. She thought it was me hiding in the bathroom. Again she saw long, dark hair poke from around the tub area. She said: "Donna, cut it out!"

There was no reply.

She stood up to look around the wall, and sure enough no one was there. She walked over to the sink to wash her hands and she spotted a pale face with vacant eyes flash in the side of the mirror's reflection. She broke out into a cold sweat and couldn't unlock the bathroom door fast enough.

This entity never missed a beat to show itself to anyone in my household. For all we knew it was doing back flips and juggling plates in front of our dad. But for whatever reason, he refused to see it, hear it or believe in it.

PRAYERS AND HOLY WATER

As each day unfolded it came with a new experience for every family member. It seemed as if this entity (or entities) that cohabitated with my family tried to make himself (or herself) known in some form or another. Our mother was a devout Catholic and her salvation came in the form of a rosary, a Bible, Holy Water and a prayer. But tragically enough it seemed as if with every psalm my mother spoke, things elevated to a new level of malevolence.

As my mother doused the floors, beds and closets with Holy Water she recited, "Our Father, which art in heaven, Hallowed be thy Name. Thy Kingdom come, Thy will be done in earth, as it is in heaven. Give us this day our daily bread, and forgive us our trespasses, as we forgive those that trespass against us. And lead us not into temptation, but deliver us from evil. For thine is the kingdom, and the power, and the glory, forever and ever. Amen."

As she recited this prayer over and over, the room's temperature would drop like we were the middle of a wasteland in a dead and icy winter. Things would seem quiet and somber for a day or two after she sprinkled the Holy Water, but then they would eventually come back with vengeance, as though to let her know that they were *not* happy!

THE OUIJA
(PRONOUNCED WEE-JA)

As a kid I remember that my mother loved a good garage sale, flea market or yard sale. She would scour the *Herald Statesman* newspaper for any local sales we could possibly go to on Saturdays if the weather was nice. She would pile the three of us kids in the car and we would each get a small allowance to spend in case we spotted something we wanted. She would make it a fun day, making lunch bags with sandwiches and *White Rock* canned soda. On one particular day we ended up at this old church flea market sale. I remember it smelled musty from all the boxes that volunteers had brought in to donate their items. It was near the end of the day and the church announced the sale would be ending in twenty minutes. I was getting frustrated because I had one more dollar left.

My mom said, "I don't know if you can still find anything here for a dollar."

I roamed up and down the long aisles with the long folding tables cluttered mainly with junk. Then, I came across a broken game box from *Parker Brothers*. It smelled like someone's attic. It was a board with letters and numbers on it. And it came with some triangular glass indicator with a hatpin through the center of it. And guess what? It was exactly one dollar!

Oh my, I was excited! I was not too sure what to do with it but it was a dollar! How great was that? I handed the old man selling it my last dollar. He looked at me with mild concern and asked, "Do you know what this is?"

I shrugged and shook my head 'no'. He took my dollar and handed me the beaten up, aged box and said, "Have fun, kid."

I had it under my arm and began to search for my mom at the homemade holiday ornament table.

"Ma, I found something for a dollar."

"Very good honey, what is it?"

As I held it up her eyes widened and she looked freaked out! "I don't think that's a good idea. Where did you get it?"

45

I pointed to the table where the man was sitting. No one was there now. He must have gone to the bathroom or left to get ready to pack up.

"I think it is very weird that someone would sell this at a church flea market," my mother said under her breath.

I didn't care because it was one dollar! And it was mine. Yup – all mine. Lucky me, huh? You see where I am going with this, right? If you ever see a Ouija board for sale, especially at a church for a buck ... I have one word for you: R-U-N!

My mother and I found my sister and brother outside the church waiting for us. They had stopped at a table where chips and soda were sold, so they sat on the steps of the church talking and snacking away. My brother saw the box under my arm and pulled it towards him, "Let me see that."

My sister's jaw dropped. "Ma, why did you allow Donna to get that?"

"She paid for it and the guy left before I even found out."

"I think we need to leave that thing here!" Doreen strongly suggested.

Hearing what they wanted to do with my game I began to throw a tantrum, "I want it!" Then the tears came flowing of course ... I never get to have fun! "I never get what I want," I whined.

My mother grabbed her head and said, "Doreen, just let's go! I have a headache. I have to get home and make dinner; your father will be home soon."

My brother said to me, "It'll be okay." Then he looked at my mother and sister, "I will show Donna what it's for and how to use it the right way."

My sister shook her head and said, "It's still not a good idea; I wish we would dump it somewhere."

I started to cry again.

My mom said, "Okay kids, get in the car, it's about to rain and we have to get home."

I was as happy as a pig in shit to keep the mysterious game that I purchased with my very last dollar! I knew it had to have been better than the vase I bought at the last garage sale. I really thought I would be able to blink myself into that vase like a Genie ...those dumb-ass shows!

The Ouija is said to bring unwanted things when not done properly and when you use it correctly it may open the door to things you don't want! Either way, in retrospect, I would say: leave it alone. It's not a toy on *any* level. It poses as a friendly, harmless game, even slightly helpful so that it can lure you in. It's addictive, I will admit. You find yourself going back to it again and again, needing to find out more and more. You will find yourself being moody, depressed and even snapping at your loved ones for no apparent reason. And all the credit will be going to your new invisible houseguest. But I did not know the above mentioned when I bought it. I was a naïve child who thought it would be cool to play with. I did not want to wait until someone had time to use it with me properly. I wanted to play with it as soon as possible.

When we arrived home, I sat at the dining room table. My dad was out. My mom was on the phone with my grandmother in the kitchen. My brother and sister went out to visit some friends. I opened the damaged, musty box. The glass indicator had a slight crack down the middle. I lightly placed my fingers on top of it and felt the indicator move ever so slightly. I wasn't sure if it was the nerve endings on my fingertips making the indicator move or some unseen force. I started to ask questions: "Are you here with me now? Is your name Henry? How old are you?"

As a side bar ... sometimes entities lie. They might say they are a child when they are not. They might say they are friendly when they are not. They might say anything to you if they believe that they can punch their way into your universe.

I heard my mom's footsteps and I heard her voice say. "Okay mamma, I love you. I'll talk to you tonight."

As she hung up the phone with my grandmother I quickly moved to throw the board and the glass indicator in the busted box and place it under the buffet table in the dining room. I knew my mom would be angry if she knew I was messing with this board alone. She walked into the dining room, "So, what are you doing?"

"Nothing, Ma," I answered as I pretended to play with my dolls as she entered the room.

"Would you like a snack?"

"Sure!" I said, and followed her into the kitchen.

Shortly after my attempt of working the board on my own it seemed as if the entity became stronger and made its presence known more than ever.

As days passed I would sneak the board back out from underneath the buffet table. I would wait until no one else was around and I would continue to communicate with the spirit(s). One night my brother was stayed home and said, "I'll show you how to use the board, Donna, if you'd like?"

He, of course, never knew I was sneaky and sat with the board already. We sat knee to knee on our dining room chairs. We each placed our fingertips on the triangular indicator. He began asking questions like: "What is your name? Why are you haunting us? What year is it?"

The indicator started to move ever so slowly. It landed on random letters but nothing that spelled any names or real words. They didn't make any sense to us at all. After about thirty minutes my mother came into the dining room with two glasses of juice for us.

"All right, Larry, time to bring this session to a close and perhaps we could find a good movie on TV instead."

We placed the Ouija board on top of the dining room table. The indicator was smack in the center of the board. We walked away to the living room, which was two feet away and plopped down on the floor in front of the TV. We kept hearing something scratching or dragging, but we thought nothing of it. Moments later we heard the sound of glass sliding. The object hit the dining room wall and shattered. We jumped. My mother jumped up from her living room chair to see what it was. It was the glass indicator from the Ouija on the floor shattered.

My mother ran to the kitchen to get the dustpan. My sister came into the room and said, "I told you we should've left that board at the church!"!

WALKIE TALKIE PEOPLE

I was about nine years old at the time of the following incident. My brother and sister had been babysitting me while my mom was across town taking care of our grandmother who had been ill. I recall my sister being in our bedroom reading as my brother decided to play with me to keep me occupied. He loved to play this game called "stunt man". He would do these Houdini-styled feats and have me keep time to see how long it would take him to escape the latest challenge or adventure. He even received Ronco's 'As Seen On TV Magicians Kit'. Evel Knievel was one of his favorites, too.

This one afternoon wasn't different than any other day in our household. My brother had a pair of Walkie Talkie's and asked if I wanted to be his "magician's assistant'.

"Yes!" I said. I was so excited!

Okay, so here is the plan (it wasn't much of a plan as I look back at it). The plan was to place one winter coat on him backwards and tie his hands behind his back, and then tie his feet to his hands. He squatted in his closet and held one Walkie Talkie "just in case".

Larry said, "Leave the room and shut the door. Count down to three minutes and listen on the Walkie Talkie in case I need you to help me."

My sister had no clue what as to we were up to. She was in the end bedroom down the long foyer reading a Mary Higgins Clark novel. I sat in the living room on the couch and I started the count down. After about one minute I heard him key up the walkie talkie, "Quick, get in here and get me out."

I suddenly felt myself freeze, paralyzed by fear. I heard the walkie talkie key back up and I heard a man and woman laughing and they said, "Donna, don't do it."

I could not move. I was in shock. I had no idea who the other voices were telling me not to go and help my brother. My brother started to kick his legs on the inside of his closet and you could hear his muffled screaming. I started to cry and I screamed for my sister.

Doreen jumped off the bed and ran the long foyer and yelled, "Where is Larry?"

I pointed towards his bedroom. She opened the closet door and he fell out. He was out of breath and looked white as a sheet. He was trembling. "It felt like there was someone in here with me and I heard someone breathing next to me."

That is when he began to really panic. Then he looked up at me and yelled, "Why didn't you come when I asked?"

I told them about the man and woman I had heard on the Walkie Talkie laughing, "They were telling me not to let you out, don't go. I couldn't move."

I felt so guilty that I had not helped my brother. Needless to say that was the last time we played that game. I truthfully believe that the entities in the home manipulated the walkie talkies, and were hoping to suck my brother into their existence and out of ours.

Some people have questioned that it could have been a neighbor on the same channel, and that they might have been having some fun with us. But my response to that is that these voices were of grown adults, a man and woman that spoke at the same time. They said my name, and they said in *unison*: "Don't Let Him Out!"

These were not human voices that I heard. I felt as if I was actually being held in my seated postion when it all took place. I know that it might sound absolutely crazy, and if I myself heard this story, I would have my doubts to be sure. But this house continuously played upon our vulnerabilty and weakness. It manipulated us on more than one occasion. No matter how much we tried at attempts for a normal life, it made sure our lives were pure hell.

THE WRITINGS ON THE WALL

School was out! I was on summer recess! I stayed up late and watched our black and white thirteen-inch TV. I remember my sister and I would watch *Mary Hartman, Mary Hartman*, and re-runs of *Taxi* as well and *Cell Block H* on that old thing. We would eventually fall asleep from exhaustion, and mom would come into the room and shut off the television.

I woke up late the next morning; my sister was already out at Cross County Shopping Mall with her friends. I heard my mom yell, "Donna, no!!!"

I scurried down the hall foyer towards the kitchen. My mother was angry with me, but I had no idea why. She thought I was playing dumb. I said, "Ma, what did I do?"

She pointed to the pantry. "How could you do such a thing?"

I had no clue what she meant by this. She was running to the sink from the walk-in pantry that was in the kitchen. "Look what you did? What is wrong with you?"

I walked over to the pantry and saw my name written in blue icing from a tube. It was written large and sloppy. "I really did not do this mom," I said, shaking my head back and forth. She stopped and looked at me. Then the situation became even scarier for the two of us.

Whatever is in this home is doing all these things. Our family just wasn't safe. This thing, this entity, was marking its territory and wasn't backing down. It was causing an increased amount of fights between our family members. Thank God my dad was recovering, and was taking a walk outside when all of this unfolded.

Was it singling me out by having my name appear in the pantry written in blue cake icing? Was it just trying to get me into trouble to have fun? What did this mean? I sit here so many years later, and I still do not know.

51

THE INVISIBLE FARM

In the summertime I was allowed to stay up a little later than normal. It was about 10 p.m. when my mother carried our black and white television into the kitchen. She thought that it would be fun to watch TV in the kitchen as we ate our snacks. My brother and sister were out at *Movie Land* on Central Avenue, so they wouldn't be home until around one in the morning. My mother made me a cup of tea and for herself – a cup of coffee. We had *Ritz* crackers and cream cheese and jelly as a snack so we could eat while watching a movie.

My dad went to bed pretty early. He kept his bedroom door open just a couple of inches but we closed the kitchen door so our talking or the TV wouldn't wake him.

I recall clearly that it was hot and humid out. My mom had the kitchen window open. The cicadas were so loud. I've always loved that sound. To me it was relaxing to hear them on a hot summer evening. We finished watching the Saturday night movie. Back in the 1970s when the 'late' movie ended the station would sign off and you would hear either a high pitch tone and see a test pattern or just 'white noise'. Mom turned off the TV and we sat there chatting away.

She looked at the clock and said, "Doreen and Larry should be home pretty soon. You'd better get to bed." The house was so still, so quiet. It was almost 1:00 a.m. I hope they are okay." I could hear the concern in her voice.

We heard my dad snoring loudly. I started to giggle. "Shush," said mom with a smile and then she started to chuckle as well. Our smiles then turned to pure fear! We heard what can only be described as nothing other than animal hooves clip-clopping in the foyer outside the kitchen. Then we heard a goat: "baw, baw, baw".

We jumped up! I screamed. My mother grabbed my hands and we carefully headed for the door. As soon as we swung kitchen door open, the clip-clopping stopped as well as the goat 'bawwing'. Looking around we saw nothing out of the ordinary. We quietly walked up the hall towards my father's bedroom. The door was completely open. I suppose that it was possible that he woke up to use the bathroom at some point earlier in the evening, but I think that we would have heard him get up since he would usually clear his throat.

We both stood in front of his room. We could still hear him snoring. It was then we felt the iciest of chills from the bedroom as if he had an air conditioner on, or it was mid-winter. What was even stranger was the odor that permeated the room. It smelled like barn-animal feces, urine and fur. We have no explanation for this occurrence.

My brother and sister came home about ten minutes after this happened. We had told them what we heard and smelled. My brother mentioned that sometimes a haunting is just a particular 'bead in time' on a loop replay, and that it just replays for no reason. It was just 'stuck' in a scientific loop of a parallel universe. Either way you view it, it scared the crap of out us.

DOPPELGANGER
DOPPELGÄNGER: A GHOSTLY COUNTERPART
OF A LIVING PERSON

My first experience, with what I have no other way to describe other than a doppelgänger, occurred on a day just like any other hot summer day for me. I was playing up the street with my friends, running back and forth. As a rule, my mother would stand on our front porch and call, 'Donna. Come home!' when the sun started to go down, and the streetlights come on.

"Ma, I have a bad headache," I said as I ran up the front steps.

She noticed my face was beet red. As we walked in the house she scolded, "That's because you don't stop to drink any water during the day. Go inside, get your bath towel and pajamas."

She ran a cool bath for me to try and see if that would help my migraine. As I soaked in the tub (for about twenty minutes) she called through the bathroom door, "Are you alright?"

I said, "Yep."

I dried myself off and threw on my cotton pajamas. When I walked into the bedroom I noticed a tray next to the bed with a washcloth soaking in a bowl of cool water, ice cubes and some witch hazel. My mom was holding two orange flavored children's aspirins for me to take, and a glass of cold ginger ale. I propped up my bed pillows as I tucked my feet under the cool sheets. The oscillating fan was blowing a slight breeze about the room.

"Ma, can you turn on the TV so I can relax as I listen to it, please?"

She sat on the edge of the bed and watched TV with me for a bit until I became drowsy. She whispered, "I will be in the kitchen, call me if you need me." She kissed my head and I heard her walk out.

The coolness of the witch hazel was comforting and I slowly drifted to sleep. I am a very light sleeper, so with any noise I wake up quickly. I always knew when someone was about to enter the bedroom because the floorboards creaked underneath linoleum vinyl tiles.

Squeak. Squeak. Squeak.

55

The floorboard squeaked as if someone were entering the bedroom. I lifted the compress off my forehead to see who it was. It was my sister, Doreen. She did not say a word; rather she simply looked at me and smiled. She was wearing this long, psychedelic silky hippy robe our grandmother gave to the both of us to share. It was a one size fits all deal. She just kept looking at me and smiling. She went around the bed and towards the nightstand lamp then disappeared! I freaked out!

"Ma!" I screamed. She came running up the foyer and I told her what I just saw.

Quite puzzled, she said, "I don't understand how this could be."

Then my sister Doreen really *did* walk into the room, but she was wearing jeans and a Rolling Stones T-Shirt. I explained the events to my sister. She went over to the closet, "Look, the robe is right here. It never left the closet." She was correct: It was still hung on the hanger!

Research I have done has revealed the following: In fiction and folklore, a doppelgänger (<u>German</u> for "double walker") is the <u>paranormal</u> double of a living person, typically representing evil or misfortune. In modern vernacular, the word has come to refer to any double or look-alike of a person. Doppelgängers often are perceived as a sinister form of <u>bilocation,</u> and are regarded by some to be <u>harbingers</u> of bad luck. In some traditions, a doppelgänger seen by a person's friends or relatives portends illness or danger, while seeing one's own doppelgänger is an omen of death.

On another occasion we experienced hearing my dad's voice. But it wasn't him at all.

My father decided to go to bed early one evening in what used to be my room. My brother, sister, mom and I were watching a movie in the living room. We were eating cream cheese and jelly saltine snacks that mom had made for us as we watched TV. After the movie ended (around 10 PM) my brother said 'good night' and went into his bedroom. My sister and I went to our room, and my mom pulled out the sofa bed where she slept. By then I had a problem falling right to sleep - I was afraid of what may happen when I did!

The house was dark and silent. I must have been lying there at least a good hour, wide-eyed and staring up at the ceiling hoping for the morning to come quickly or perhaps for another family member to also wake up. That would be a perfect excuse to get out of bed and be with them so I wouldn't be alone. Suddenly, seemingly out of nowhere, what we all heard next was frightening and captured everyone's attention: my father's voice shouted loud and clear, "Bury the dead in the incinerator."

My sister and I jumped up and screamed. We heard a commotion in the hallway (my mother and brother running into each other trying to come into our bedroom). We shut our door and moved the dresser in front of it shaking all the while. We didn't know what to make of it. My dad never got up after he said that. The four of us ended up falling asleep from exhaustion. The next morning dad tried to get in the bedroom. The door hit the dresser and he yelled, "What the fuck? What's going on?"

"Do you remember what you said last night?" my mother asked him through the closed door. He had no recollection, and thought we were all nuts. "You people are full of shit already with this crap!"

He got dressed and we heard the front door open and close which meant he went out to get his daily paper. We moved the dresser and came out and then changed our clothes so my mom could take us to my grandmother's house across town. We spent the day there and came home around 6 p.m.

My mother asked my dad again if he remembered; he said, "No Marge! Now cut the shit already. We can't move. We don't have money right now. What are you pulling?"

My dad, I must say, had a real hard time accepting that these paranormal beings really did exist and lived with us. We were prisoners here. Some homes have spirits that just exist and cause no harm. Others are evil and want to drive the living insane and take their souls. This home vibrated such darkness, such sorrow, that you began to feel it too.

JAIL HOUSE ROCK

My mother and brother were huge Elvis Presley fans. They had every one of his albums and were devastated when they learned of his passing on August 16th, 1977. We piled into the car to go to our grandmother's house. We were celebrating my sister Doreen's 19th birthday when the news of Elvis' death put a damper on the whole thing. No matter what radio station we turned on, or TV channel we flipped through for the remainder of the day, they just kept repeating the death of The King of Rock N' Roll.

My grandmother had a beautiful cake ready for my sister and we sat around Doreen as she opened her gifts. My sister had a date later that day so we wrapped up the visit to get her back home in time to get ready. She was going out to dinner and a movie. As we arrived home my brother also 'jetted out' to play basketball at the high school with his friends. My father – as usual – was tired and went to bed.

My mom and I decided we would sit on the porch, taking our two glasses of soda with us. I remember the sky growing dark gray and the branches were blowing upward. The wind was picking up a bit. After about thirty minutes mom said nervously, "I think we'd better go inside, it's getting too windy to sit out here." She always feared getting struck by lightening and the storm was moving in very quickly at this point.

"I'm getting worried about your brother on the basketball court."

"I'm sure they stopped playing by now," I assured her as we passed through the dining room toward the kitchen. As we passed Larry's bedroom, which was directly outside the dining room, we heard a snippet of the song "Jail House Rock".

Okay, I know that sound - *The Warden threw a party in the county jail. The prison band was there and they began to wail!* And that was that! No more! Poof, it stopped. We stopped dead in our tracks and ran into Larry's bedroom. The door had been left open. There was no radio left on, no radio alarm clock set, no TV left on. Why did it happen on this of all days? It's as if this entity was acknowledging the death of Elvis, and making us aware is was there with us once again … like it ever left our side?

Once again there was no scientific explanation for this incident. My brother stopped to get a quick burger before coming home, and as soon as he arrived we told him what we heard coming from his bedroom. He shook his head and asked us question-after-question. He asked us if we checked the radio, the TV, the alarm clock, was his window was open, etc. This was in the hope that we might have mistakenly heard a car passing by, playing the music that we had heard. The window was closed, we reported. We had no answer. It was just another puzzle to add to the others that continued to plague us.

THE INDIAN CHIEF

I believe that our ancestors try to contact us, and try to pay back any grievances. It wasn't long after we moved in that I started to see an Indian Chief appear to me. He was in full-blown headdress and warrior paint. It's not so much what he said but he was gritting his teeth and his eyes were stern. I heard him screaming garbled animalistic grunts and yells. He was filled with anger and hatred. I noticed he resembled my father a lot.

"It's just your imagination, Donna," said my mother.

I saw the whites of his eyes and felt the breeze his feathers made as he moved around the room. This was not my imagination at all; it couldn't have been. I would need to 'locked away' or tested in a government lab if my imagination was this good!

One afternoon I was laying down with another migraine headache, I got them frequently as a child and still do as an adult. I was in bed with a cool Witch Hazel-soaked cloth draped onto my forehead. I could not sleep, the pain was too intense. I heard this jingling sound – almost like small bells – and out of nowhere I heard a man's voice chanting and screaming in some ancient tongue I knew nothing of. I looked up and saw a man in complete Indian dress, with bright feathers and war paint across his face looking furious with me. I screamed at the top of my lungs, "Mom!" The Indian faded into nothing as soon as I heard her footsteps coming closer to the bedroom. I was crying and terrified.

He looked like my dad only with long silver hair and dark skin. His eyes were piercing green. His mouth was open in a snarling way as if he was telling me something or confirming something I was supposed to know. I could see every detail of the headdress: the bright feathers (many were white with touches of yellow and orange placed in between the white ones) and his tan-colored hide Indian dressing, fringes and all.

I told her what I saw. She said, "If you see him again to count to ten." She hoped I could control this hideous mirage in some fashion.

I hated to be alone in this house. I never knew what was going to happen. I never knew when the Indian or the dead boy would show up. The moment I was left alone I would feel a cold sensation that was unmistakable. The hair on the back of my neck would stand on end and I had a strange feeling in the pit of my stomach. My heart raced and I became traumatized in such a way my school grades were getting lower and lower. The teachers would send home notes asking if things were 'okay' at home.

I hated to sleep. I hated to be left alone. Yet I became socially disconnected from other children. Other children did not have 'ghosts' in their homes, and furthermore when I spoke of these experiences to other children I soon found that I was being told not to come over anymore.

I was home from school one day and my mother had to do house work. She asked me to play in the kitchen at the table and she would hear me if I needed her. She turned the vacuum on in the living room and I sat with my dolls and my lunch in the kitchen. I turned to look at the doorway of the kitchen when there he was: long, white 'crazed' hair from underneath his feathered headdress. I cried out, "MOM!"

Finally, after a few times of me screaming bloody hell, my mother heard me over the noise of the vacuum. She never actually turned off the vacuum; she just dropped it and ran to me. Again he was gone. This was a cruel joke.

It was almost as if I was the only one meant to see this Indian Chief. "I saw him again. He looks just like daddy."

"Do you know that you are Native American? Your father's ancestors were Mohawk, and there was bad blood in the generations that followed. It had something to do with land and women." Of course being so young, I never knew this information about my family background.

"Maybe you are 'open' to the spirits and they are trying to convey a message back to the family." Who really knows why I was seeing this Indian? And was an ancestor of mine really trying to settle a grievance? Once she told me this I did not see the Indian again. But when I close my eyes, decades later, I can still see what he looked like. It's as if this house opened a portal for this spirit too, to come through and show itself to me.

DISEMBODIED BOOTS

It was very early on a Saturday morning, maybe about 5:45. I could hear the birds chirping and I knew my parents would get up soon. The sun began to rise and spray light through the bedroom curtains. We had switched to vinyl roll-down shades since the Venetian blind incident. My sister was still asleep and I heard our dog Sammy snoring in his dog bed which was next to ours.

I was afraid to get out of the bed. I guess that typical feeling all kids get when they think there is a monster living under their bed. But in our case, I was probably right! When I got out of bed I would actually stand up *on* the bed and leap from it to the hallway. And to get back in bed I would run and jump into it really fast. My sister hated that. I can see where that would be annoying while she tried to sleep. Operative word: tried.

I heard my mom get up and shuffle into the bathroom, then from the bathroom shuffle into the kitchen to prepare the coffee percolator. Then I heard my dad follow behind, shuffle into the bathroom and clear his throat really loud as he always did. I began to smell the coffee perking. I loved the smell of coffee in the morning, and it made me feel comforted. Even though I was way too young to drink it, I still loved smelling it. Sometimes my mother would make a really weak milky cup for me so I wouldn't feel left out when sitting with the adults.

Since both my parents were both up I felt safe to get out of bed. I stood up and leaped over my sleeping sister and landed in the hallway, which were approximately three to four feet away. My dad yelled from the kitchen, "Would you cut the shit out!"

I wasn't exactly graceful when I landed; there was usually a loud banging sound as I hit the floor. He just did not understand the severe phobias I was developing, all born from the fear of all these supernatural experiences I was going through. Another thing my dad never understood was that this house was haunted. He thought we were all going crazy and he never believed, or at least never owned up to believing. He would rather have thought the whole family was having a mass hallucination instead.

It was now 7 o'clock. I had some tea and toast for breakfast and then I watched television until I was allowed to go out at nine. I kept telling my mom, "I am SO bored. I want to go out and see if my friends up the block wanted to hang out."

"Donna, be patient," she pleaded.

After nagging the crap out of my mother about going out, she finally said, "Okay, if you promise just sit outside on the porch or the wall until 9."

"Okay, I will mommy," I said excitedly.

I sat on the L-shaped gray stonewall that needed a lot of repair after so many years. As I remember, the distance from the wall to the house was perhaps about twelve feet, so our 'yard' consisted of partial grass, dead grass, and some tulips that Tony Valeria's sister (named Graciella) had planted.

I brought my bright red Radio Shack AM/ FM transistor radio, that had a black plastic handle, out with me. I thought I was 'the shit' with that radio. Ha! My dad had taken us one Saturday afternoon to Radio Shack and bought all three of us the same radio. I used to love to listen to WABC AM. Harry Harrison would play the Top 40. Well, so much for my transistor radio. As I was sitting listening to The Captain & Tennille's song, *Muskrat Love*, I heard heavy-footed heals walking behind me coming from the driveway. I casually turned my head to see who it was. I was not expecting what came next. I quickly wished that I stayed inside my house at this point! When I turned to see who the footsteps belonged to, I saw two black boots. No body attached. And they were making their way up toward me from the long, concrete driveway. I dropped my radio and it broke apart when it hit the cement. The batteries went rolling into the street and I felt as though I were moving in slow motion. I couldn't get up the front steps fast enough! I banged on the door and rang the doorbell in total panic.

"What is wrong?" My mother opened the door looking startled at me.

I was out of breath and shaking. I calmed down enough to tell her. She was beside herself.

This thing, this entity, this dark being ... was now visible and able to show itself (themselves) to us outside the home! This thing was both confident and arrogant.

"My radio is broken and it's still outside. Can you get it for me?" I said as I grasped for self-control. I was too scared to go back outside. Mom ran outside. "Don't tell dad that you dropped it." She would later ask my brother if he could fix it for me before my dad found out.

With the broken radio in hand, she said, "Describe the boots again."

"They were long, black leather, farm type, kind of old fashioned boots," I explained. I also told her I thought they were large and assumed they belonged to a man. I can still see them plain-as-day even now in my mind.

What was I seeing? Was it an old farm hand doing his chores in another dimension? Was it Henry? Who the hell knows? But I can sit here today and honestly say that you don't need special equipment to see or hear these spirits. They wanted us to notice them. This was *their* home and they were never going to let us forget either.

If I owned that house today I would have a doormat that says, "No K-2's or EMF's needed here" ... **<u>Enter At Your Own Risk!</u>**

EXIT WOUNDS

In 1979 we were asked to vacate the home by Tony Valeria. He knew that my dad had suffered two heart attacks and was on disability and social security. He also knew that our funds were limited and he wanted to raise the rent to an amount that would be impossibly high for us. I found out that we had to move and I cried because I would be losing whatever friends I made over the last five years. It was already incredibly difficult for me to make friends; in the 1970s it was not fashionable to be friends with people who see dead people!

We had three months to find a new home. In one way I was elated because we would be getting out of Dante's Inferno. I definitely suffered emotionally from living there being tormented by these spirits. Constantly 'attacked', I became an insomniac for most part of my childhood. Living in such a horrific location for so long set me into a depression. I began overeating to compensate for what bothered me and the lack of sleep and the feeling sad all the time.

When you live in such a haunted place, you are like a sponge. You are the battery of energy for these souls to use, especially if you are a young child. Without any question I believe your health suffers.

My mother begged me to stop talking about what the family was going through after she was asked to come in and speak with school officials who suggested I seek therapy because I was crying in class and making up these crazy stories about ghosts in our home. It was bad enough the local church turned their backs on us in a time of need. No one understood or believed us. So I had to keep it all in and never speak of these beings anymore. Maybe a fresh start, a new school, a new apartment would be a good thing? Who knew? With a fresh start maybe we could be a normal family again.

THREE MONTHS AND FIVE DAYS LATER

We were settling in our new apartment. Boxes were everywhere. My brother, my sister, my mom and I were in the new kitchen eating lunch. My brother took our wall phone receiver off its hook and started to dial our old phone number at Lee Avenue. As he held the receiver up to his ear, his eyes popped out and he held the receiver out for my mom to hear. She passed the receiver around to listen.

Someone on the other end had picked up the phone and we heard a many voices, like there was a party going on. Men and women were laughing, and then it went to static, then nothing. The line went dead. We dialed the number again and got a generic recording: "This number is no longer in service." We had dialed the correct number, it was the Yonkers exchange followed by 0665. Were we hearing the spirits in the house?

We discovered that a new family moved in about five months after we moved out and that they stayed only one month. Then Tony Valeria's two sisters passed away. He moved to the West Coast and he died soon after.

ALL GROWN UP NOW WHAT

The years that followed have left me with this sensitivity to the unseen. Shortly after I enter a room I can often sense if something supernatural may have entered.

But why do we feel we are being watched when no one else is in the room? Why do we sometimes feel like there is a fun-house effect in some rooms and not others? Why do we get nauseous in some locations and not others? I have tried to look into the scientific reasoning behind theories. I learned that if you are in a location where there is an abundance of electrical wiring you will have a high EMF (Electro Magnetic Field) reading.

Sometimes you will get both that feeling of being watched and also being sick to your stomach. I have learned that sometimes the fun-house effect occurs because of an uneven foundation in the home or uneven floors that have been warped from humidity and age.

Once you rule these out entirely, yet you are still left with the same experience, then you may have yourself an authentic haunting.

When people go through the multitude of paranormal experiences, my suggestion is to try to rule out every possibility. You want to debunk it first before you claim it's haunted. (If you went around claiming you see and feel spirits everywhere, people would really think you've lost your mind altogether!)

The next thing to do is obtain a full history of the location: names of owners, relatives, etc. Find out if anyone passed away in that location or how deep their attachment was to it. Sometimes spirits get stuck because they are just not ready to move on. Maybe they are waiting for or looking for a loved one? Or sometimes there are spirits that remain because they just don't realize they have died! Occasionally they need a little nudge. They wait for someone to communicate with them at times to deliver a message to someone. Speak to them as you would a living person.

Try and remain as calm as you can. Breathe and ask questions. Try and reason with the spirit. You can help others by giving them closure and move on to where they need to be.

In the past I have been able to sense if someone was either about to pass, just passed or stuck on our level and perhaps had unfinished business. It's in that moment you realize there is something bigger than all of us. This is why I feel it is so very important to acknowledge the living and our loved ones now. Don't wait until you lose someone to get a message to or from them.

We are all energy and energy never dies. It just changes form. With all the books you will read on this subject, all the shows you will watch, all the investigating you will do, we, as investigators, have yet to scratch the surface of what we are trying to figure out. So this will always be an ongoing process.

I highly suggest to those who have gone through these experiences to keep a log or a journal. Follow it. Make mental notes of other signs you perceive as messages. It doesn't always have to be an obvious sign either.

As a younger person I was always told not to speak of these things. I was told people will think I am crazy. Well, I am too old to really care what anyone thinks of my theories on the paranormal. I know what I saw, heard, felt and my family also lived through these things along with me. I have nothing to lose. In fact sharing my experiences has been therapeutic for me and hopefully has been able to help others as well.

Some call me different because I welcome these experiences like a spring day. Each one is new and different like a fingerprint; for there are many layers of existence to our complex universe. I think it's no stranger than the duties of a surgeon, a homicide detective, or an undertaker. It takes a special kind of person. The love I have for the paranormal is like a mother loving its child. You can use your paranormal experiences as tools to build on and embrace it.

What used to frighten me has now enlightened me. I embrace rather than run from it. I feel as if I have been given this opportunity to assist those in need to help them move the deceased on to their next level of existence.

Until we meet again, be well my friends.

LEE AVENUE REVISITED

Thirty-three years had passed since I had stepped foot on the front porch of the home that nearly drove my family out of our sanity. The question though: "Was I ready for what was or wasn't about to happen?"

I knew as I grew older (and my parent's passed away and my brother passed away, leaving only my sister and I) that I could not wait any longer before I told our story. The answer was simple: Write the book.

In 2012, I released The Lee Avenue Haunting. It came out with a humble quietness. No fanfare. I self-marketed this labor of love. I believed in it because I wanted to share our experiences, and possibly help those in need or let others know they were not alone in dealing in things of sensitive nature. Six months after the book was released I was still doing book signings at local Tri-State area 'hot spots'. I called City Hall of Yonkers, New York, and I requested the most recent owners' names for "Lee Avenue". They told me. I wrote a gracious letter that included my name, the title of the book, and my contact information in the hope that they would contact me. I waited and waited. Nothing. I never heard back from them.

One day, my friend, Donna Davies (whose is also an author of several books) invited me along to share a stand with her at Sleepy Hollow Cemetery in Tarrytown, New York. It was October 27th, 2012 to be exact. I can't forget that date because that marked my the twentieth anniversary of my mother's death.

It seemed fitting to honor her in this way.

The day was overcast, but not cold for late October. It was just cold enough for a warm hoodie, and if I had only remembered to bring the chairs for Donna and I to sit in!

Other than that, the day was perfect! The autumn leaves were falling like slow motion orange and brown confetti.

The "Headless Horseman" even paced back and forth by our stand several times. We posed with him and fed the horse apples. It was like a

Halloween snow globe of magic.

So many people stopped by our stand and seemed to enjoy asking us both about our books. They asked for signed copies and to take pictures with us too.

It was a very surreal and sweet day. I was proud and happy to share an experience that once had marked a reign of terror for my family, and that now presents the promise of help to others and the admittance of experiences in a time that is now acceptable. When these thing's originally occurred, no one believed us or they had a terrible time accepting belief in what were telling them.

By four thirty that afternoon the gates were closing up and Donna and I were packing up the stand and loading up her car. As we sat in her car, we decided to drive down to Yonkers and stop by the house and see if the new owners would be willing to talk to me in person.

I was nervous. I have to honest. There were so many factors in play here. First, was the house.

Would the porch swallow me up and drag me to hell? (Smile) Second, would the new owners call the police on me and have me arrested for stalking? But I knew one thing. I would kick myself if I never tried. So we ventured off to Yonkers from Tarrytown. Of course a stop by a local coffee shop first! About an hour later we arrived in Yonkers, New York.

Donna pulled up in front of the neighbor's house and she said, "I will stay here ET". We call each other "ET", which is short for Evil Twin because both of ours names are Donna, we both write, we both love Halloween. You get it, right?

I felt a bit of sweat under my arms, and my hands began to shake a little as I approached.

My knees buckled just a bit simply from looking at the house. I felt like the Lion in the *Wizard of Oz*, looking for courage. I did notice they had painted the front door a bright red. Churches often do that to keep evil out. I thought to myself, "how odd", but let me not jump to conclusions.

I noticed a car in the driveway with a blondish woman exiting it. I walked up the door and I rang the doorbell. A man came to the door. I said: "Hello Are you Mr. McDermott?"

He said, "No, but that his sister is behind you." He had an Irish brogue. A woman came out of the apartment that I used to live in with three children trailing behind her: a little girl, and two small boys. They all had on Halloween costumes on I would like to point out.

Another interesting fact: my family had three children two girls and one boy.

Also, the family before us, the Nigel family, had three children two boys and one girl.

Our landlord from whom The McDermott's bought the home had three sibling's, two girls and one boy.

The woman behind me was the sister-in-law to the woman who answered the door. And the man who answered the door was their upstairs tenant. He had moved in where my old landlord used to live. Mrs. McDermott told me that her husband was not at home at the moment, but asked what I wanted. I shook her hand and introduced myself. She covered her mouth and said, "Oh yes" in her Irish accent "I got your letter earlier this year. My husband thought it was a joke and threw it away."

I replied, "no mam' it's not a joke, I am real. I took out my driver's license to prove to her I was who I said I was. I also gave her a copy of the book, and I asked if they had any paranormal experiences since buying the home. She said they purchased it three years ago in 2009. She looked around a little nervous because her children were standing there. . She said, "No, no, no, nothing has ever happened."

I told her that I was also a paranormal investigator and that I would be interested in investigating my old home if possible.

She looked at her sister-in-law and they both said that they would not mind, but Jerry (her husband) would not permit it. So the fact that she would have agreed to it leads me to believe that she may believe that something is going on but cannot admit it. They came here and put all of their money into this one house. I guess are afraid of losing re-sale value and possibly getting a bad name for themselves. She said her husband was dead set against the whole thing.

I realized I was causing an uncomfortable situation at this point. I was lucky the porch did not swallow me up, and no one called the police. So I told her that if she ever changed her mind to call me. She agreed. I gave her a copy of the book. I asked one last favor: That I might be able to photograph the house as it stands today. She allowed me to do so. It was decorated for Halloween fittingly enough!

I snapped approximately ten pictures, then I got back into the car and told Donna all about what transpired on that porch. She said, "Well, at least you got that far ET!"

True!

So there you have it folks, I went back to Lee Avenue and although they claim not to be bothered, I am receiving many e-mails from others who live in Yonkers, New York.

They are people who know about or have lived on Lee Avenue. They are coming forth with paranormal experiences. So I do believe it was that area which was reported farmland? I believe it has to be connected.

Thanks for sharing my journey back home.
Peace, DPB

PHOTOS

The Parish family photo was taken with my grandmother, my parents, my brother Larry, and sister Doreen for my grandmother's birthday in 1978.

PHOTOS

Me in my communion dress taken on the side of The Lee Avenue house in 1975.

PHOTOS

Me with my parents in front of Saint Paul's Church on the day of my communion in 1975.

ABOUT THE AUTHOR

I was born and raised in Yonkers, New York. I remember, as early as the age of three, having experiences, but not as severe as the experiences that my family and I experienced residing at Lee Avenue.

I was raised Catholic, however I did part ways with the politics of the Catholic church. I felt they fell short in helping my family when we dearly needed them so.

After doing some research about different spiritual religions, I decided that Wicca was a path that I would take.

I love animals and find myself to be a advocate for animal welfare. I dream of owning and operating an animal sanctuary to assist with resolving the issues with homeless animals. But until then, I will be the voice for the voiceless and help in whichever way I possibly can.

I am working on my next book, *Growing Up Paranormal*.

Made in the USA
Charleston, SC
19 September 2014